100 T-SHIRT DESIGNS IN 1 HOUR
MODULAR DESIGN FOR MERCH BY AMAZON

BONUS
Giving Shirts a "Vintage" Look

by Tyler Yates

CONTENTS

Introduction 3

Step 1: Open Up Microsoft Word Or Any Word Processor. 4

Step 2: Open The "Snipping Tool" 5

Step 3: Repeat Steps 1 & 2 With Different Text 7

Step 4: Making Designs Merch-Ready 8

Bonus: Giving Shirts A Vintage Look 16

INTRODUCTION

So, you applied to Merch by Amazon and you just got accepted. Or maybe you've already been active on MBA but you really want to start pumping out more designs to tier up or increase revenue. Either way, this is the book for you.

I'm going to show you a couple of little "hacks" or tricks that you can use to quickly turn your ideas into products. Personally, I like to do things the laziest way possible because that allows me to really maximize what I get out of the time I spend working. I bet you are like that, too.

These methods are not rocket science, and I'm sure many graphic designers and Merch sellers already use them, but I think this could be a great guide for anyone new to the idea of thinking "modular."

First, you need to have an idea for a design that people will want. When I was in San Macros, TX last summer for the Float Fest music festival, I saw a girl wearing a shirt that said "Body by Tacos." I chuckled to myself, imagining a fitness program like Weight Watchers with the same phrase or a similar one. It was then that I went *eureka!* ...Not out loud of course. I realized that people are interested in this phrase and like it enough to purchase it.

I made a note of this in my iPhone using the handy-dandy Notes app (I have hundreds of entries in this app; I've never needed more than the stock iOS notes app), and I sat down at my computer the very morning after getting home from Float Fest.

I know the title of this book says "100 designs in 1 hour", but technically I made 161 designs in 82 minutes[1]. I just didn't think "161 designs in 82 minutes" had the same ring to it. Please note that this works best for text-based designs, but there's no reason you couldn't add graphics later. Here's how I managed to pull it off:

---

[1] I checked the timestamps of my files in windows explorer: First design at 12:01 PM and last at 1:23 PM. I know that's not morning but cut me some slack, it was the weekend

STEP 1: OPEN UP MICROSOFT WORD OR ANY WORD PROCESSOR.

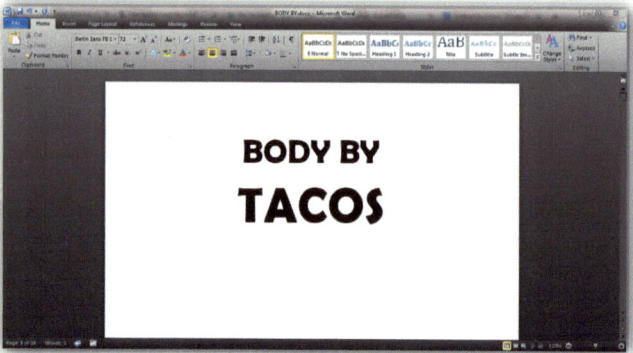

Figure 1. The First Step.[2]

What you want to do is use Microsoft Word to type out as many combinations of your phrase as possible, preferably in the font that you want to appear on your final product. At the very least, this is excellent for rapidly prototyping and saving your ideas. Remember, we want to do this the laziest way possible since our goal is to churn out ideas. Be sure and click the "align to center" button on your word processor and set the font size as big as possible to fit nicely on the screen. You want the words to be large to avoid pixelated designs later on.

---

[2] Here I'm using the font "Berlin Sans FB Demi" because…it looks totally rad, bro! Jokes aside, I chose it because it's already in the default fonts.

STEP 2: OPEN THE "SNIPPING TOOL"

Ah, the snipping tool, a formidable asset in our arsenal of laziness. I remember when I would use "Print Screen" and paste into MS Paint when I needed to take a screenshot. Those were the caveman days; welcome to the future! Go to "Start" if you are on Windows, and type "Snipping Tool" into the search bar:

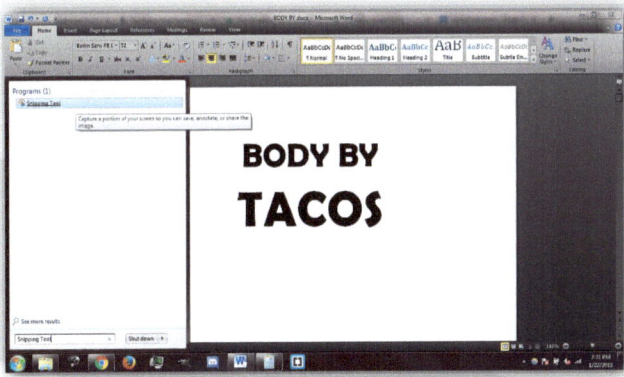

Figure 2: The Wonderful Snipping Tool.[3]

"New" should be selected by default and your screen will be greyed out. Click and drag to make a box around the text for your design (the edges don't have to be perfectly spaced, just get as close as you can to the letters).

---

[3] If you are using a Mac, you can use [Shift + Command + 4] to do the same thing.

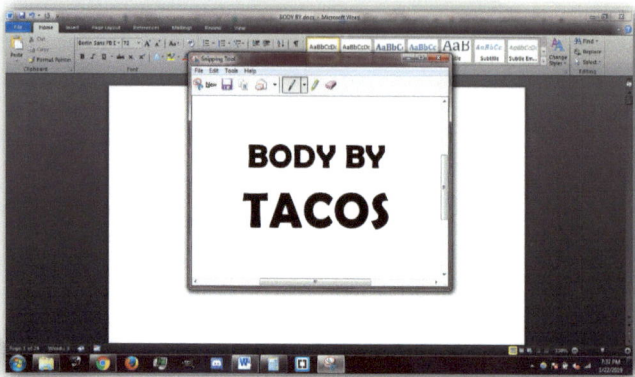

Figure 3: Screenshot of Your Design

Great! You're already almost done with this one. Click the floppy disk icon to save the screenshot, give it a good name (mine is "bodybytacos.png" because clearly file names must be creative) and make sure you save the file as a PNG.

STEP 3: REPEAT STEPS 1 & 2 WITH DIFFERENT TEXT

This is pretty self-explanatory. Go back to your previous file (mine is just called "BODY BY.docx") and change the last word! Take a screenshot and save as PNG. If you like brainstorming as much as I do, you'll quickly have dozens of files like this:

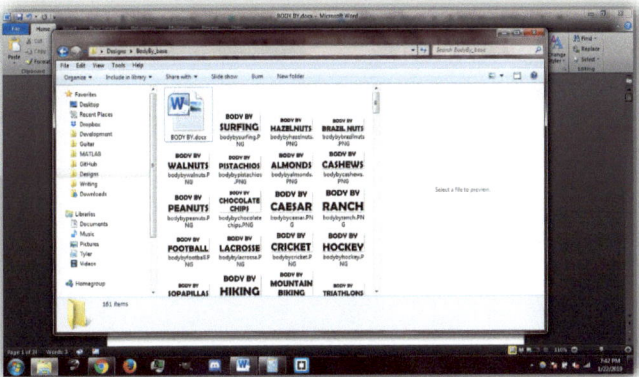

Figure 4: Dozens of Designs, the EZ Way

Keep this up as long as you like, or until you run out of words and ideas. When I first made the "Body By" designs I was on tier 100, so I knew 161 designs was enough to fill my MBA slots!

STEP 4: MAKING DESIGNS MERCH-READY

If you are using MBA, you must download and use Amazon's product templates. These can be found at https://www.merch.amazon.com/resources. If you are new to MBA, there are instructions on this page for using the appropriate template. I personally use GIMP, which is free for both Windows and MacOS.

Since we are making designs for T-Shirts, open up the "Standard 4500x5400" template from Amazon. Your screen will look like Figure 5.

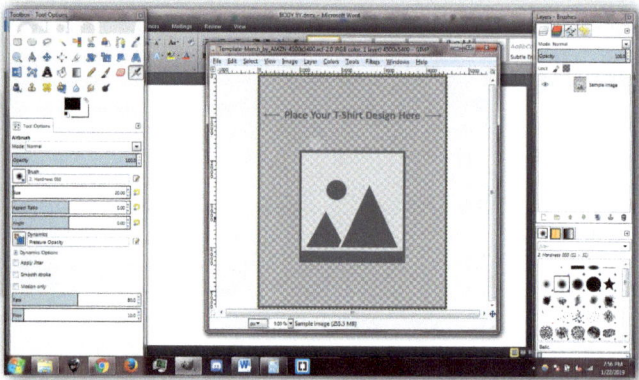

Figure 5: A New Hope, Er, Shirt

Go to File > "Open as Layers" as shown in Figure 6.

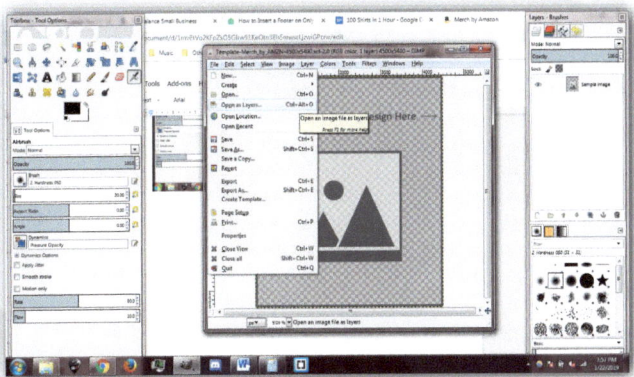

Figure 6: Open as Layers

Navigate to the PNG file of your design. In my case, the file is "bodybytacos.PNG." Open it and it will appear in your GIMP project.[4]

---

[4] If you use Photoshop, you probably already know how to open and use layers. You know, since you're fancy enough to use Photoshop. At what Merch tier does that start, again?

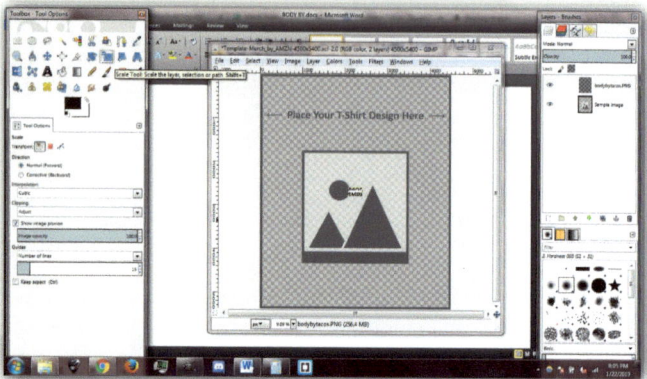

Figure 7: You're Gonna Need a Bigger Design, Bro

As you can see in Figure 7 above, the PNG file looks pretty small in the template. To fix that, we're going to scale it up with, you guessed it, the Scale Tool (highlighted in Figure 7).

Click in the center of the "Body by Tacos" image (make sure you are on the appropriate layer or nothing will happen), and the scale dialog will pop up, as shown in Figure 8, below.

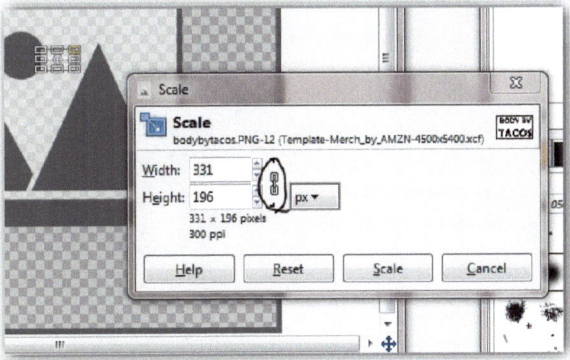

Figure 8: The All-Important Aspect Ratio Button

Click "scale" then click and drag on either the width or height up arrow until the image is the size that you want on your product.

If you did that right, your image will probably be hanging off the edge of the screen, and will not be centered. We will use the "alignment tool" to re-center our design. This tool can be tricky if you've never used GIMP or similar programs before.

Click the "alignment tool", then click the design image, then click the arrows for centering vertically and horizontally. These are shown below in Figure 9.

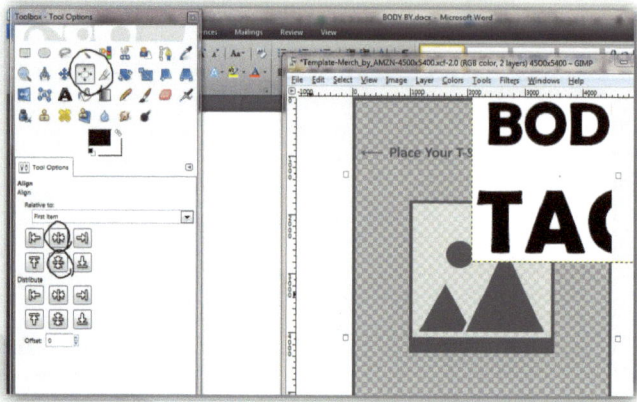

Figure 9: Designing and Aligning

Usually I will use the "move" tool before the alignment tool so that I can position the image freely vertically, then use the alignment tool only for horizontal centering. That way the image will be on the upper part of the shirt when you submit to Amazon. This is pretty simple once you do it a few times.

Next, you need to hide the base layer by clicking the eye icon shown in Figure 10, then find the "fuzzy select" tool (often called "magic wand" in other programs) circled in Figure 11.

Figure 10: Hiding the Base Layer.[5]

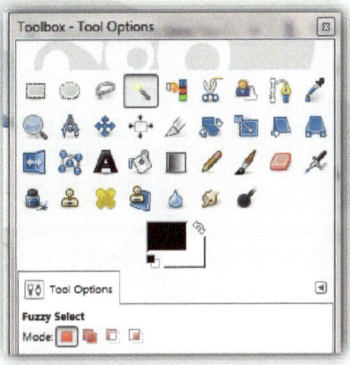

Figure 11: The Fuzzy Select Tool

---

[5] You could hide the base layer at the beginning or end. All that matters is that it doesn't show up in your final design.

With the fuzzy select tool selected and the base layer turned off, click anywhere in the white area and press the delete key on your keyboard. Delete the white areas on the inside of the letters, too (Figure 12).

Figure 12: Fuzzy Deletion

Once all the white is deleted and your background is just the checker pattern (that pattern indicates alpha, or transparency), I like to go to File > Save As to save the GIMP file just in case I want to come back to it.

You're done! All that's left now is to go to File > Export As, give the file a name, and make sure it is exported as a PNG. Exporting will show a green loading bar, and once it's finished, your design is ready for sale on Amazon!

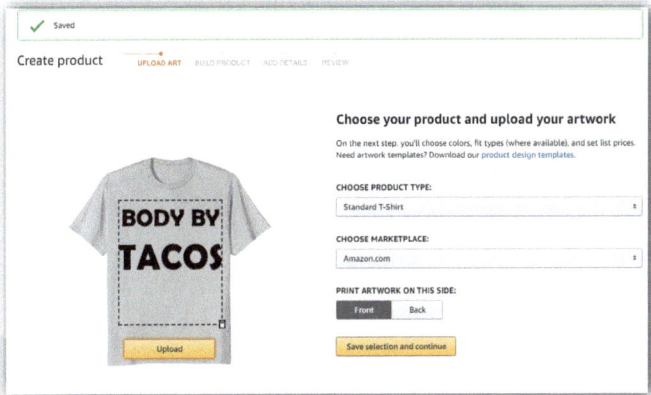

Figure 13: The Finished Product

Congrats! When you reach your upload limit for the day, you can polish off the other designs you created in Steps 1 & 2 by repeating Step 4.

BONUS: GIVING SHIRTS A VINTAGE LOOK

When I made the "Body by" set of T-Shirts, I knew that they looked a little too plain. I mean, some people might think the wording is funny, but simple text doesn't always cut it. After countless internet searches and a couple YouTube videos, I figured out a simple way to "distress" your t-shirt designs, giving them a "vintage" appearance. My manifesto for making shirts look "vintagey," if you will, follows.

BONUS STEP 1: FIND AN IMAGE OF CRUMPLED PAPER

You read that right. It doesn't sound very clever, but search online for a picture of crumpled up paper; use the word "texture" to avoid getting a ball of paper. The more creases, the better. It would be best to use a public domain image to avoid copyright issues, and I am not a lawyer so I'm not going to tell you to just use the first picture you come across[6] on Google. Somebody worked very hard taking that picture of crumpled up paper![7]

BONUS STEP 2: ADD CRUMPLED PAPER AS LAYER

We are going to open the crumpled paper file just like we did with the "bodybytacos.png" file. You are then going to scale the image to completely cover your design using the same methods as scaling the design image.

---

[6] Using this method, it would be very hard to tell what the original photo was anyway. But hey, we are trying to sell t-shirts, and we don't want any bad marks on our Amazon account.

[7] Please understand it's been a long night of writing and I need to make these jokes. Also know that I care a lot about copyright since I make products, too.

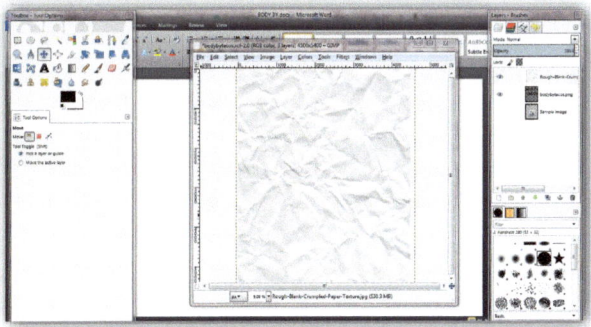

Figure 14: The Paper Texture

While the paper texture layer is selected, go to Colors > Threshold as shown below in Figure 15. Drag the arrows circled in Figure 15 until they are on the edges of the curve in the threshold graph, or until you like the way the texture looks, then click OK.

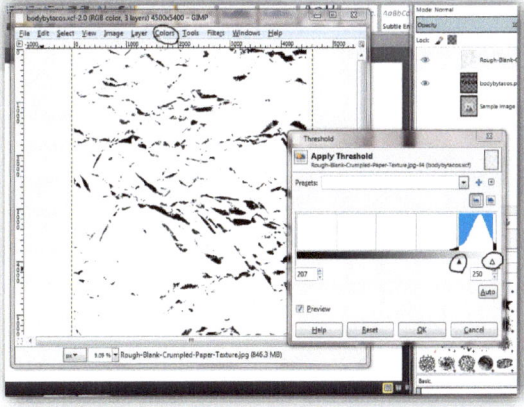

Figure 15: Setting the Threshold

Next, click the fuzzy select tool and click anywhere in the white part of the texture. Go to Select > Invert so that your selection will invert to the splotches of black in the image.

Switch layers to your design image, and press the delete key. Click the eye on the paper texture layer to hide it, showing just the distressed text like in Figure 16.

Figure 16: Hiding the Crumpled Texture

Deselect, and you're done! The finished product is ready to be exported and added to a shirt on Amazon. Congratulations and happy selling![8]

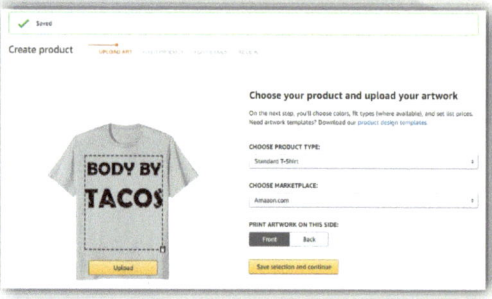

---

[8] I know this is a great example but I would appreciate it if you don't steal my designs. Think of any phrase that can be changed by one word! Thanks for reading my book 😊

www.ingramcontent.com/pod-product-compliance
Lightning Source LLC
Chambersburg PA
CBHW040352220526
45473CB00009B/2864